FOREST BOOK

FOOTPRINTS OF THE
MATEJA MATEVSKI

MATEJA MATEVSKI belongs to the post-war middle generation of poets which formed during the 1950s and marked a decisive turning point in contemporary Yugoslavian poetry. He was born on 13 March 1929 in Istanbul into an immigrant working class family, but after his birth they moved to Yugoslavia. He spent his childhood and the war years at Gostivar in Western Macedonia and then studied Yugoslavian literature at the University of Skopje. He then spent a year in Paris studying French Theatre. His career has been varied. Having worked as a teacher, and in radio and television, he became a critic and later editor of the literary programme, working his way up to become Director General of both radio and television. He is currently President of the Macedonian Committee for Foreign Cultural Relations and is now Professor in the Faculty of Drama Studies at the University of Skopje. He is also a member of the Academy of Arts and Sciences in Macedonia and Principal of the Arts department. He is one of the founder members of the International Festival of Poetry Evenings at Struga.

Matevski started writing in 1950 and has become well known internationally for his translations and his poetry. His first works were published in France as early as 1959. Apart from winning numerous awards in his own country, he has also received the Special Prize for Mediterranean Literature at Palermo in Italy, the Blaise Cendrars Prize at the International Poetry Meetings at Yverdon in Switzerland and has been decorated by the French with the Légion d'Honneur. His volumes of verse have been translated into many languages, but until this volume, English translations have appeared only in anthologies or reviews.

EWALD OSERS is a native of Prague but has lived in England since 1938. Among his published works are translations of over 90 books (24 of them poetry). He is also a poet and a volume of his own poetry has been translated into Czech and was published in Prague in 1986. He has also lectured on translation internationally. His awards include the Schlegel-Tieck Prize 1971, the C.B. Nathhorst Prize 1977, the Josef Dobrovský Medal 1980, the Goldene Ehrennadel des BdÜ 1982, the Silver Pegasus of the Bulgarian Writers' Union 1983, the Gold Medal of the Czecho-slovak Society for International Relations 1986, the Dilia Medal, Czechoslovakia 1986, the Order of SS. Cyril and Methodius, Bulgaria 1986, the European Poetry Translation Prize 1987 and the Pierre-François Caillé Medal in recognition of his service to the translating profession.

NIKOLA MARTINOVSKI (1903–1973) was one of the founders of contemporary Macedonian art.

FOOTPRINTS OF
THE WIND

FOOTPRINTS OF
THE WIND

Selected poems
by
MATEJA MATEVSKI

Translated from the Macedonian
by
EWALD OSERS

Drawings by
Nikola Martinovski

Photographic reproductions by
Blagoja Drnkovski

FOREST BOOKS
LONDON ☆ 1988 ☆ BOSTON

PUBLISHED BY
FOREST BOOKS
20 Forest View, Chingford, London E4 7AY, U.K.
P.O. Box 438, Wayland, M.A. 01788, U.S.A.

First published 1988

Typeset in Great Britain by Cover to Cover, Cambridge
Printed in Great Britain by A. Wheaton & Co. Ltd, Exeter

Translations © Ewald Osers
Illustrations © Nikola Martinovski
Jacket design: Andy Jones, A. Wheaton & Co. Ltd.

British Library Cataloguing in Publication Data:
Matevski, Mateja
Footprints of the wind: selected poems
1. Title   II. Osers, Ewald
891.8'.191   PG1195.M36

ISBN 0–948259–41–8

Library of Congress Catalogue Card No. 87–0827876

This translation has been made possible (in part) through a grant
from the Wheatland Foundation.

Forest Books gratefully acknowledge financial support for this
publication from the Arts Council of Great Britain.

Mateja Matevski

The poems in this volume come from
Mateja Matevski's collections:

Дождови (Rains) 1956

Рамноденица (Equinox) 1963

Перуника (Iris) 1973

Круг (Circle) 1977

Липа (The Lime-Tree) 1980

Раѓане на трагедијата (The Birth of Tragedy) 1985

Contents

Introduction

The poetry of Mateja Matevski brings together several of the main strands of Balkan poetry. The precise depiction of particular details of the natural world — the 'astonished snake/lying in the grass/ ... coiled by thunder', and the 'clumsy beetles crawling/over dry leaves' — reflect the realistic tradition of much twentieth-century writing. The vivid imagery and musical construction of the poems remind one also of potent symbolist influences and of the devotion to verbal harmony so typical of this region exemplified in the lyric poetry of Peyo Yavorov at the beginning of this century.

There is, indeed, a strong element of folk song in many of these lyrics, which sometimes fuse ancient with contemporary rural scenes, as in 'Sunset', where the 'flock enamoured of the shepherd's pipe' could as well be grazing in Bion's Thessaly as on the pastures of today. From time to time one is reminded of Lorca whose vivid symbolism derives as much from folk beliefs as from his brand of surrealism, and Matevski's world of nature often possesses a Lorca-like dramatic intensity and inventiveness, as in 'my day crumbles/in the sun's embroidery hoop'. It also contains that heart-chilling directness and simplicity which is characteristic of many of the songs in the folk tradition of all countries; 'Vision', for example, ends hauntingly with the lines, 'She dissolved in the daylight/in the garden/ in the distance.'

A sense of the mysterious and the numinous attends these poems, but it is combined with an earthy sensuality that prevents them becoming vague and dreamy. Thus in 'Nirvana' the 'delicate mist raised by the sun' is followed by the much more immediately sensual statement, 'the rain's warm water/rouses/the leaves' eroticism', while in 'Roots' the precise details of the first stanza are counterpointed by the more diffuse universalities of the second, the two moods of observation and reflection being fused at the poem's conclusion.

There is also an epigrammatical element here, but it is the epigram of the riddle and the folk saying rather than that of the sophisticated wit; it has the pithiness of country lore rather than the contrived concision of the Greek Anthology. 'Who is he that walks/on the ashes/of time' is a stanza that undercuts all cultural differences and speaks directly to all humankind. It reminds us that the language of poetry is, or should be, one common to us all and transformed into poetry by its music, its pattern, and its sudden surprising clarities, as happens in 'The Ballad of Time' where we read: 'in falling water/you can't swim.'

These poems, grounded firmly in precise observation, and in a deep sympathy with common speech and an understanding of folkways, nevertheless have a symbolic and romantic power which is astonishing. They pierce through the very world of appearances upon which they dwell so affectionately, and while the speaker may dwell upon tree, grass, bird, and river, he tells us also that 'we escaped through the sky of appearances/on wings of the wind with the colour of the bird/and the song of the snow.'

It is in lines like these that Ewald Osers' mastery of the translator's art reveals itself most clearly; the words are musical, their pacing exact and harmonious, their organization of consonant and vowel deft, so that these poems from another language emerge as English poems in their own right. The compactness is never too compact, nor is the texture too dense. The voice is always a speaking voice with its natural pauses and hesitations, its sudden leaps and its slow deliberations. His version of 'Early Apostrophe to Autumn' recalls the music and sensuality of Keats' great ode, but there is not the slightest hint of pastiche, and the third verse paragraph of 'Lime Tree' has a helter skelter urgency and conviction that stem directly from his manipulation of open vowel sounds and thrusting consonants.

One is, of course, reading here the poetry of Matevski–Osers, as one reads the poetry of Cavafy–Mavrogordato or Homer–Fitzgerald. In such fusions of voices neither voice is betrayed, and cultures are brought together in amity and illumination. The great translators are the great unifiers; in their work we discover and share concerns and visions, delights and disorders, comedies and tragedies common to us all. We also discover significant differences. At any one time the writers of one culture are likely to surpass the writers of another in some particular. Indeed, a tradition moribund in one culture may take on life in another, as the sonnet form, no longer vital in English, has been renewed in the many sonnets of the Hungarian-Canadian George Faludy.

Mateja Matevski's poems, by way of Ewald Osers, renew much. Here we have a poetry of the natural world and of the relationship of humankind to the whole power of creation that is now rare in the English language. The world of this poetry is a system of connections; everything touches and connects with everything else and there is nothing inanimate in the universe. The 'flock of stones' grazes 'silently on the hand of time', and the moon ' 'converses with the tipsy air', while 'enraptured leaves are in pain' and 'living sand' 'insatiably devours the riddle and the answer'.

This is not the 'pathetic fallacy' at which we have sneered for so long. It is no version of either pantheism or animism. Indeed it comes close to the observations of some recent theoretical physicists, and to the Gaia hypothesis of Dr James Lovelock, in its recognition that life is common to all that exists, and that everything is not only a part of everything else, but a functioning part.

Thanks to Ewald Osers, Mateja Matevski's poetry has now become a functioning part of poetry in English, and I, for one, as a maker of poems and a reader and teacher of poetry, am delighted.

Robin Skelton
The University of Victoria
Victoria, B.C.
Canada

Translator's Foreword

Macedonia (Makedonija) is the most southerly of the six republics which make up Yugoslavia. In the west it borders on Albania, in the south on Greece, and in the east on Bulgaria. Macedonian is a Slav language, more particularly one of the group of southern Slav languages; its closest relative is Bulgarian.

Today the territory which made up ancient Macedon, the kingdom of Philip and Alexander the Great, is divided between Yugoslavia (i.e. its Republic of Macedonia), northern Greece, and southwestern Bulgaria. It was the speech of Salonika, in 'Greek Macedonia', only a few miles a across the frontier, that became the first written Slav language — known to linguists as Old Church Slavonic. In the 9th century A.D. two brothers, Cyril (also known as Constantine) and Methodius, monks from Salonika, were invited by Rastislav, the ruler of Greater Moravia (on the territory of present-day Czechoslovakia), to Christianize his people and for that purpose they translated the Gospels and various liturgical texts into their native Slav idiom.

Macedonian literature, Matevski argued in an interview given to the publisher of this volume, is therefore at the same time the oldest and the youngest of all Slav literatures. During the Middle Ages, for a period of 550 years, the territory of Macedonia, like the rest of the Balkans, came under Turkish rule and Slav writing survived only in the monasteries, though the living language, of course, continued to be spoken by the people. Not until the 19th century, with the stirrings of national awareness throughout the oppressed peoples of Europe, did a rebirth of Macedonian as a literary language begin. But even then the emerging writers, notably Konstantin Miladinov, all used their own local dialect. Only with the end of the Second World War and the Yugoslav War of Liberation, and with the establishment of the Macedonian Republic within the Federative Republic of Yugoslavia, in 1945, did the literary language begin to be codified.

Today, Matevski says, all literary genres are being practised in Macedonia: poetry, drama, the novel, the short story, and criticism. World literature is being translated into Macedonian — from Homer, Dante and Shakespeare to the moderns — and Macedonian literature is being increasingly translated into other languages. He himself has done a lot of translating, from French, Spanish, Russian, Serbo-Croat and Albanian.

Asked about the melancholy note that is present in all his poems, Matevski referred to the wartime experiences of his generation and the difficulties in the early years after the war. As a child, he explained, he had moved from the countryside into an urban environment, and nostalgia for nature had always remained with him. Yet his images of poplars and stones, of the river, the lake and the sea should not be taken as purely impressionist landscape paintings but as objects he identified with, as symbols of existentialist concerns.

It certainly was the compelling nature of these often bleak and arid images and their mysterious nature, the irrepressible optimism of the flowers springing from an inhospitable soil, and the wistful paradox of the firefly whose light dies in the brighter light of the day, that first attracted me to these poems.

I should like, in conclusion, to record my thanks to Zlata Kufnerová for her invaluable help with these often difficult and opaque texts.

Ewald Osers

AUSTRIA

HUNGARY

ITALY

ROMANIA

● ZAGREB

YUGOSLAVIA

● BELGRADE

BULGARIA

N

Adriatic Sea

ALBANIA

● Skopje

F.W.—B

The Poems

Illumination from the 16th century Gospel by Saint Mateja, Lesnovo, Macedonia.

The poplar

Green fountain-jet balanced in silence
sadly erect and peacefully upright

Children crumble
the nests of sounds
and yet it's so hopelessly alone

Lean, support yourself, you innocent
on the wind's shoulder
Don't bend, rise up for one brief glance
across that uneven
tall
waving meadow of houses

Then awake the gorge
from its red grasses:
they remember the soil
that gave you birth

Threshing floor

Yellow suns splashing
on the firm threshing floor
under the hooves of hunger

Dark concentric weights
rustling above the ripe landscape
which weeps in the sparks of grain

Wild whirlwind of young hopes
dreaming of brightly-coloured sounds
the wind's wide song

Huge cargoes of the day
crawling down the long road
of tears and laughter

Crimson. Crimson. Crimson.

Like a song carried off
into the blue sea
of mountains
the sunset
drowns . . .

From grass to shepherd's pipe
from flock to cloud
all luxuriant
inflamed

From breasts to song
from step to fountain
all phenomenal
and pampered

A flock enamoured of the shepherd's pipe
a bell lost in a song
an eye crazed over a peony

Crimson. Crimson. Crimson.

Moon

O flat meadow you bitter delight
The nocturnal sun has risen on the mountains
the cloud doesn't frighten it
the wolf doesn't chase it away

Snow sweeps the footprints of the wind

Silence is pecked by blind birds
in winter
from Christmas to Epiphany

What a night is this a real
night up to the shoulders
what a dream is this a real
dream up to the knees

Dogs are barking
wolves approaching
brides gird their breasts
with tufa

Under the window howls the night frost
a frightened bird freezes
tucked in its bosom

Oh don't approach
sweet frost from meadows deep in snow
we've waited so we'll wait again

O flat meadow
you bitter delight

Cold

On my forehead lie
the shades of night
by the cold stone
my day breaks

My dream exfoliates
in sleepless nights
my day crumbles
in the sun's embroidery hoop

The earth holds me
the cloud carries me
and the stone escapes
from my deaf soul

In vain you call
In vain you seek
the blue doves
of years

Cold February lying in your breast
is frozen like a spring howls like a dog

Voice

My voice has come from far away
like hastening autumn
like a neighing horse

If you find a lump
reach a lump of earth
it won't accept you
into black sorrow

From suffering you
become a voice
from waiting I
a deaf chamber

Your breath goes far
uprooting me here cursing me there
your dream hastens in the distance
desiccating me in sweet shivers

Two distant cypresses
on the cliffs of dream
lonely we wave
our wind-arms

Road

Night
like a blocked chimney
is dark and sooty

Mists are the smoke
of burnt dreams
in the soul

The invisible road is my longing
gone astray
in the empty fullness
of the dark

I am
a smouldering star
one which the road has in no way
exhausted yet

And night
and the road
and the longing within me
are remains of something
still to come

Return

You're coming to me and I sing
of your non-return

From azure heights
from deep shadows
with years
with suffering

Why are you hastening
with your dying
through slow living

The earth has long absorbed
my song
my curses

Deaf time is not awakened
even by love's howling

The heart has forgotten you
only the wrinkles on my face
remember you

On my face
on your rock-face

Spring song

Now the leaves are turning green
now birds fly and old wounds bleed
by fences in the fields

Snow is swirling in the wind
sadness settles in my heart
down the highways down the roads
calls the distance

By the fence a horse is neighing
to three hills it will be running
three far hills beyond returning

Cuckoo's call ringing
from blue on high
Oh treacherous spring

Snow is swirling in the wind
by the fence a horse is neighing
Down the road lies misty distance
distance beyond all returning

The fence

Even the bird returns voiceless
from that fence
and the wind which ceaselessly blows
from me to it

The stone is bored under the grasses' green rust

No one can tell
what lies behind it
It's so high
I can't see beyond
It's so near
it doesn't exist

Always crouching before it
I forget myself
shackled by its
lost shadow.

Love

The high sky's on fire
above the low scrub
the forest's on fire in the spacious halls

Through fern tangle through fire-charred thicket
a flock of springs is
running romping

Young birds in the dew
snakes in their hide-out
under the stones

Why are you watching me why are you grieving for me
from the upper halls
from the tall windows
I throw you an apple
you expected a stone
I forged to the fence
you tied to the window

The forest's burning in my roaring breast
I embraced the thorns
of your roses

There's no refuge for your grief
for your grief and my laughter
only the forest burning in the upper halls
only the sky on fire above the low scrub

F.W.—C

13

Concert

Saint Sophia

The voices blend in the air
like forest smells
birds sing into your ear
but you don't look at them
you only look at the scarlet noonday
under the sunlit forest
while the wind waves to you
with the weary wings of the corn

The angel descends from the wall
and brings you wine
but you're drunk already
with bread
Who will remember this music
for which the walls here live
upon whose dewy foreheads
are carved
cages of beauty

Everything rushes out
in noisy ecstasy
and everything hurts inside
in quiet excitement

The music crashes from all sides
like waterfalls of sound
into mysterious pools

Entry into the garden

The garden opens to the rain like a bloom to a glance
in which lives the forgotten world of what's fulfilled
Don't wake the seeds which sleep deep down
in the earth's darkness
The time will come for their roar
spread by the roots' rainbow
Entry into the garden is a slow entering
into the trap of time
which only the word can open
Catch it in the wind catch it in the painful root
of beautiful things
before it speaks to you in the language of insects
which draw their cloud over the roses
Their scent is mingling with the rainbow's colour
that lives in the dream's darkness
until some variable weather enters the garden
to uproot it
to raise it up
and blow it over the leaves

The word is not yet born but already
it's giving birth
all about

Shadow

I thought I'd accompany you
along time's distant wanderings
to the springs of the wind
to the roots of the flowers
My goal was the horizon unlocked by your laughter
beyond which vanished your bird-flock of words
You were like a poplar growing out of my heart
which dispels the dark clouds on my forehead
Your tremor was the sparkle of dew
upon your leaves on my breast

For a long time I thought I'd accompany you
on your beautiful intentions of aimless movement
but I've realized that you're real only
in my nightmarish dreams
which fill the circle of my existence
All else were footsteps following your shadow
beautiful as the shadow of the sun
and like the rainbow's delicate face
which stays alive
while the dew lives

Vision

She appeared in the morning light
in the garden
in the garden
in the distance

With a nightingale in her heart
with an anemone in her bosom

Wind is lifting me
from all four sides
from all four sides
amidst black nightmares

With a stone in her heart
with a viper in her bosom

Cloud is prodding me
laughter has died in you
eye does not regard you
dream doesn't find you

With starry face
with dewy strawberry

She dissolved in the daylight
in the garden
in the garden
in the distance

Height

The bird's long flown away
the flower has wilted
the rain is lost

Noontide is silently enveloped
in sunlit contemplation
The wind sweetly gathers
the forest scents

A stone has gently rolled
into the water

And after many centuries I saw
in its trembling
the rocking of
a distant shore

The rock

Bloody plumage of screams descended
on the dusty stone
An astonished snake
lying in the grass
is coiled by thunder

The sky is steaming
The woodruff's yearning

Only the rock silently guards
the spring
from its gullet

The bird's dying
and all round
birds are singing

Loneliness

Time's swallowed time
water its source
beehive the sky
nightingale the silence

Forest has fled into forest
the appletree's moved away
stone has buried stone
couch-grass the marigolds

Down the trail of silence
the wolf slowly pads
the smoke's shadow cannot be smoothed
upon the snow

Time's sown forgotten words
into space
the valleys are echoing
sadness

And I'm far from you
with a lump in my chest
between us grows the mountain
of our sleeplessness

The ballad of time

I listen to time dying

By the leaves that are falling
by the frost biting my hands
how far have I got

It dies in everything that's born
and I'm forever smaller than it is
if only by one step

Autumn is prodigal in dreams
though sometimes sad
in falling water
you can't swim

November's rich mists
what do they feed the rivers with
How far shall I get
in their shallow waters

I listen to time dying

In autumn in this chill
a single fruit remains
asking with frost-blue lips
how far shall I get

Nirvana

The rain is pouring down
like a woman in her bath

Over the birch of her body
over the lime of her face
over the rose of her pubes

Delicate mist raised by the sun
and returning to the sun

The rain's warm water
arouses
the leaves' eroticism

and a word like a full breast
lies upon deaf insomnia

Field

O sadness of the quiet hues of longing
Green shades of willows
imperceptibly stirring
on the calm river
the creeping river
the sleeping river
embracing

Why are my eyes veiled
when the sand smiles at me?
When the daydreamed flock
from the field
gazes at me in astonishment
and the little shepherd girl
waves her hand at me

O sadness of childhood left behind
how you call me back
to your drowsy
depths

In the church

By the church door two novice nuns
and two prayer-books.
Two children selling candles.
From the altar: resurrection.
Two crutches on a concrete floor.
A lot of candles, a lot of whispers.
Resurrection.
Two crutches slipping on the path.
The children sleeping by their candles.
Two rosy-cheeked young nuns
are joyous at the resurrection of the prayer-books.
One imperceptible glance
from the cold pavement prays for resurrection.

Two crutches on the cold church floor.

First night

Moist cry of lips
and sharp permeation
of the fruit
of a new being

Small branches whispering
broken in their shadows
the Moon's curved arms
and the cloud's shoulders

A bow of sweet nerves
is tickling and playing with
some violins

The bright eye of the quiet
night
and long eloquent
silence

Stones

There's a distant mist
where stone grows like a rose
and the rose turns to stone

Through the falling dusk returns
the flock of stones
from grazing silently
on the hand of time

The bird flying over it
leaves its shadow
on the fragrant woodruff

The moon's forged its red-hot legs
while it converses with the tipsy air
It would rather chase the fireflies' trail
but cannot rid itself
of the moss's embrace
which whispers its name
in sad ancient songs

The grass knows its name
but has no word to utter it

Grass

Filled with curiosity I made for that hideous landscape
of iron scrap and concrete
and yet I survived

Now I am a small meadow-patch
of strangers' tempting hopes
for which so faithlessly I steal the river's wind

Countless journeys I offer
to eyes and feet
which wearily tiptoe over my scythed stubbles

I too have memories
but I wilt as soon as they whisper
that once I was the brilliant wing of beauty

The brilliant wing of youth
in the root of shallow waters
which linger as a yellow memory in the stacked hay.

Distant voices

From your song
to my shadow
time has spread
infinity

You sing to me softly
you're heard far away

Darkness is falling around me
the sea is extinguished for me
your voice petrifies
in my sight

Rain

The rain rustles
like clumsy beetles crawling
over dry leaves

Pale lanterns
tremble
on bare twigs

This isn't autumn ruling
but under my fingers
swirl the leaves of time
like leaves in a garden

Gently they settle
on my body's humus
on my mind on my senses
on the fruit of the earth's crust

and make it spin along
with autumn
with the rain
and the sounds of the night

Roots

We left our roots behind
by the far rivers
we left them behind under the stone
under the cloud under the dream
oh how we left them behind
under the corn under the flower under the oak
under the nightingale's plaint

We fled from them with the shallow words
of our age
we fled with empty day-dreams
with lies
with deceit
setting out secretly and hurriedly
we escaped through the sky of appearances
on wings of the wind with the colour of the bird
and the song of the snow

Bewitched we roamed through promised distances
we roamed through the rain over hilltop and rock
so we should come tired to our sleeplessness
that has lain locked behind the sun's grill

The wild olive

I watch as that dry branch is struggling
from a gnarl in the bark
from its hardness
to squeeze out a blossom
A flock of birds confusedly gazes at a rustling leaf
Time suddenly erupts thickens surges up from the sap
which inaudibly rings with spring
in its veins
A miracle occurs and the old bark
sprouts tiny wisps of foliage
like screams of winter birds
perishing far away
The olive merges with the spring blossom
of the trees
and waits
for its fruit
And that slowly appears in the small seeds of the wild
                                                    tree
which adorn its parched body
And while all round the fruits are swelling
it is flooded with longing for an unfulfilled birth
Only its perfume like a distant cloud
of jasmine lemons lilies
of the most beautiful flowers
is slowly wafted under the low branches
where it mingles with the boundlessness of longing
and the delirium of a barren spring
With it you now inhale
the beauty of the miracle of spring
and the deaf tumult
of your grief

Early apostrophe to autumn

Autumn you've fallen on two leafy hands
full of the setting sun
and the rime that's born from the sweat of dawn
urged by the whip of your windswept words

Now you're calm and bright with colours
which you release like rosary beads into boredom
into your vigil for a day that's totally yours
that will be greyness and a long dark void

But this wait's in vain   Yours won't be
any more than that tree there that's undressing
even if you strip it naked beyond satiation
it'll stand insatiable and upright before the frost which falls
on its bare shoulders

And only I can hear your speech   In soft nostalgic spasm
enraptured leaves are in pain   I bow to the trunk's root
as to a wondrous woman whom we never understood
in her insatiable play for satiation
with lone young shoots of people

Hungry and unsated are you and I
Helpless in the dark you ceased to stand
before the tall hollow tree which sways
frozen and lonely yet it does not bend
before the heavy hoarfrost of your windswept words

Helpless and empty I fall with every leaf
For ages I've been falling and shall not return
and autumn stands before the darkness of my setting
an upright brittle tree before the youthful shoot
of that nostalgic departure without return

Yours and mine

The lake

After many a year and many a dream
I again returned
to the lake
with the sweet waters
hidden in the hills' loins

The sun's diamond's
still cutting it

Not a stone in its depths
nor grass to obscure its throat
under the waves
nor the bird with its prey

I'm only an eye the eye of the sun
that ruffles its ancient
waters

Oh leave me by this lake
leave me there
by the bitter lake
dead

The birth of the firefly

Oh you who stop only when darkness stops
child of the dark of silence
of the gentle wind through sleeping grass
you whom only the stone's muteness recognizes
where do you roam in your slow delirium
as if in a fever of light
what deep-dark spots do you try to light for me
when with your light you scatter even darker darkness

You are created by the night's blind darkness
which stumbles over the wakeful rock by the silence
Oh beautiful love of that instant
illumined by curiosity
oh fate of transient beauty
of light of ages before my awakened eyes
oh magic meaning of light
which dies of light alone
but is alive so long as night is alive
so long as darkness embraces it

Rains

1.

Fear

They arrive weary they arrive exhausted the horses of space
that distant surmised rumble of forgotten talk
Ceaselessly lonely they trample under closed windows
lost they trample with unshod feet
on you oh slippery beautiful earth oh peaceful earth
they trample blended in darkness

Oh where before this cotton-wool mass
of horizon without outline
before this dark flesh of earth and night
that solid flesh firmly kneaded
by the flood of eyes and the death of space

Where oh where shall I go oh roaring and boundless sea
you monotonous
exhausted horizontal expanse
eager for the whirlwind's clean-up
Where oh where
you thick dough of rain and earth
shall I go
stones in my hands and dirt in my eyes

2.

Song

From where oh where do you come you familiar
                                        unforgettable
song you hopelessly naive child you
missile of grasses and mud birds
you dry and endless footpath through the rain
silvery footpath playful viper
where are you leading me

Always surmised in water and in darkness
sweet mane and coarse mane
considerately bold
always the gristly flesh of earth and night
sharp mane unquiet sword of light
on the silvery footpath of space
like a lightbeam like lightning

Oh carry me off carry me off my childhood
carry me off you poem eternal unforgettable age
you greatest illusion without metaphor
rigidly open eye sharp eye and deep
for all eternity's colours

Carry me off through this rain winding footpath
so you can tenderly return me to that little harbour
to that soft home of dreams

3.

Horses

They arrive weary they arrive exhausted the horses of space
(pale rains aimless and mute)
at my hands' feeding-troughs on the window

Sate yourselves I cry sate yourselves you're
sweaty and damp from the hot steam that rises
from the night's flanks

Play wildly till I shout
Start up your bird with the forgotten wings
slim-legged girl dancer you exhausted mare
let's leap through this window
together and then let's return
without ever halting
through the translucent shade of space

The lime tree

I.

When I decided to cut it down
while I was still deciding
my forehead was bedewed with hailstones
my heart beat in my throat
for parting wasn't easy
felling my contemporary the one I grew up with
whom I watched from a tender shoot to a full-grown
                                        trunk
with whom we played ring-a-ring-of-roses
I was its support and it was my swing
it sent me skywards
and I shielded it against beetles and ants against
                                        woodworm
But its growth was faster and mightier than my own
and it undermined my house
with its long deep roots which reached out
to dig through my sleep
in sleepless nights walls were cracking and doors
foundations crumbled and the roof burst open
all from its roots and branches
That day I weighed my love and weighed my fear
which froze my blood
I tested too the sharpness of my axe
for the bird in its throat

II.

First I climbed up as if in childish game
half to caress and half to kill
trying to embrace the old lime-tree
but my body turned to a cleaver, an axe
chasing the fleeing tree across the clearing

I ran on till I caught it till I clutched it
as wearily it surrendered to treacherous hands
like an exhausted kid like an overcome bird
and the branches began to drop off and leaves to fall
and the sap was mingling with tears and sweat
trickling to the ground to the bottom of my grief
where we found ourselves in a tight embrace
on the grass flattened by the heavy timber

both of us hacked about without tops without branches
with severed body stacked into piles
while nests were flying about without their birds
without their shadows without our shoulder-blades
in the air's abyss uprooted and unsated

III.

I'm lying in the grass gazing at summer clouds
to where my glances used to run up through the
                                     lime-tree's shade
which is still quivering in my memory of sky and dream
The house now stands freed from the birds' burden
tranquil foundations on dead roots
no walls shaking and no doors rattling
from tempestuous growth or the air's arousal
Now all is quiet in the space of my vision
which is learning to creep over wilting grass
instead of climbing the trembling foliage

All is quiet and calm while we two are lying
two trunks cut down two objects in pain two dried-up
                                       springs
not visited by birds nor cradled by song
Because in cutting down the tree I cut myself in half
turning my body my hand into a corpse
no longer stumbling down the road of smoke
And on the grass's edge I'm watched by the reproach of
                                       veins
with a linden fragrance
about the house and summer

Tracks

I went out into the fields
over the rustling leaves
through the autumn wind

My hope is high
at this season of fruits
and wild beasts

But suddenly after the scent
of wild animals
snow started blowing
over the dry earth

That cursed misfortune of lost tracks
warmed by the sun
smoothed out by the wind

Drifting thus in the circle of my black thoughts
I fail to grasp that in this whirlwind
not even I can be tracked down by them

The island

Suddenly to find yourself surrounded by vast water
strange water
at night without harbour
A motionless body not even rocked
by the moon
Creator of hopeless silence
of quiet
a lonely island on a lonely planet
not even a voice can help
not even a shout
across a land without past
Solitary as at the world's creation
when you must start on your uncertain walk
that leads to yourself
Raise yourself raise yourself on your hindlegs
like the forest of the lost island
which waves to the vast deaf ocean
awakening it
for some new light that can't be seen
but heralds an as yet unknown sense
a new sense
Beyond the horizon of memory and intellect
beyond the despair
of this new existence

Piercing

Who is he that walks
on the ashes
of time

Wind
night
a lost thought

Who thinks of things
carried away in
the darkness

Not even grief will help
or deceptive hope

To walk like that as though on living sand
which insatiably
devours
the riddle and the answer

Afterwards all looks equally
expunged
and forgotten

If it weren't for that piercing pain
which hurts
without declaring itself

The bullet

This bullet so carefully manufactured
from a lump of heavy ore
into a cruel grain
in some country
in some place
this bullet this wild beast
this dark messenger of death
which memorizes every letter of my name
traces my ancestors
hounds my shadow
this bullet which seeks me in the universe
which penetrates my sleep
which buries itself in my fear
without reason without asking without by-your-leave
a grain merely on its way
to its target
from the muzzle-flash
to the shattered skull
This bullet from an unknown hand
from an invisible eye
from an unperceived breath
that wants to take the breath from my body
when it discovers me and hides under my forehead
it will kill no more

On the subject of Ulysses

To return from far away
after days and years
after created after perfected horror
as if from outer space
from orbiting through darkness
through emptiness
To disembark
step on an earth that spins with stars deep inside it
from conquered emptiness
into another that awaits you
like love

The sea no longer obediently roars
under your oar
but sea-monsters and sharp rocks on the shore
still lie in wait
Only the surf of unextinguished hope of youth
whips up your blood
sets the course of the stars

And you move you move with but one roar in your
                                               mind
discovering yourself in space
having lost your way in your own sea of dreams
as in a wood
while a sweet shudder of the unknown
runs over the vast sea's skin

Your mind which knows that to travel
is better than to arrive
unlocks the words' closed cages
and a song is born
And when after so many oars and voices drowned
in the treacherous waters
the dawn settles on your face
with white hand drawing the long-sought space
upon your forehead
know then that it is time

Time you spoke up with a new tongue
before the eyes of the world
with the new words
for which it's thirsting
before you cross the familiar threshold
of rocks and monsters
the blood's dark threshold
Threshold of song
and story
with which you enter into life

Snow

Where are now those hands so gentle
which caressed
that open book
Outside the window snow is softly falling
and the barefoot flakes
are filling every nook

Where are now those hands so pale
which closed
so many books in their time
Or are they already fired with inspiration
labouring over
new lines

Where are they where? I'm waiting waiting
for them to flutter
over the book that's lying
abandoned, but instead the wind alone
in the dry leaves
is sighing

Her gentle hands are gone are gone
The question's ringing in the throat
hopelessly

Outside the answer's snowing snowing

Snowflakes are swirling swirling
ceaselessly

The Aztec calendar

A stone transformed into the sky
survives the defeated
and those who defeated them

It won't crash down
neither on the sky
nor on the earth
For it cannot walk
but only speak

Signs carved long ago
by ancient hands
move over human heads
confusing the mind

Villagers come with secret faces
to read the future
of corn
to unravel
the mysterious paths of rain

Raped earth vomits
stone and bones
pointing a bloody path
out of cries and sweat
and the rainbow of hope
which is not extinguished
any more than the sun-stone
that mirror of the sky
and legend

Eagle, snake and cactus

Let all be ruined
let all be forgotten

Fear of ancient gods
scatters ruins
wheezing and smoke rise up
on the startled wind
In the night of misfortune
let all be buried
let only the evil of gold
be unearthed
And ancient faiths and songs and phases of the moon
the lament of the Mayas and the terror of the Incas
Before the lances of the white gods
the ancient calendars are extinguished
with the ancient stars
and the seasons are enveloped
in the blackness of time
And new litanies before new temples
on the ashes of ancient books ancient maps ancient
                                                    gods
and new words before new prisons
while the fruits of the wounded earth cry up to a
                                            hopeless sky
But soon they learn about the delusion of power
the flimsiness of chains
of fetters
for the grandsons the long forgotten grandsons
are unearthing the long buried gods
the locked-up languages
the long silent songs
and eagle and snake and cactus
once more pick a spot for the cradle of song
unchain old myths among the mountains' thunder
and slaves carrying known and unknown seeds
once more move towards the great seed of the sun

Auschwitz

That flame that smoke on the snow
and that frost-clear sky
That wind of human dust
still moaning in the bones
Our own bones too are still burning here
on the pyre which never dies

    A time which even time cannot forget
    before death's chilly wall

Tears from eyes which don't exist
cry from a throat that is not
an attempt to burn even thought

    And a new rumble gathering
    to repeat your smoke
    and cinders
    and lament

    Death being perfected
    with new instruments of grief

To walk past or to stop here
chained by the cold of a long-past winter that's coming
Stop with eyes lowered to the ground
with a gaze across the wire
You stand on snow of ashes
in which still smoulders our dark defeat
of humanity

    But winter birds pecking at unextinguished grief
    at wounded memories
    ceaselessly still
    herald the spring

The knife

The root sucks from the blood
darkness and sleeplessness
Don't let the knife
repeat
the hatred of iron

Neither in the bloody
branches
growing
in the sky's
delicate womb

Nor in the eye of the nostalgic
nor in the dream

Bury it in oblivion
whence there's no return

Leave it
to befriend only
the rust of time

Transformations

Autumn's collected its fruit
Everyone's gone on his way
A rainbow like a delightful cobra
trembles in the liquid light

Leaves are falling into our eyes
tomorrow they'll disappear under snow
Rain with slow steps
walks over the dry land

The world hides in a fog
you feel deceived by illusion
the sun's still washing itself
on fruit from the very last branch

The day is filling with water
amidst solitude and dark
The fruit juicy
amidst a wilting life

On the subject of Icarus

Not at all
towards the centre
of that warm swamp
of the sky

Swarms of bees
settle in his wings
A bird that thinks
An unfamiliar mote
in the eye of the sun

Madness they'll say
but also great courage

He rises
he rises
towards his crash
unconcerned with his shadow

The birth of tragedy

When Aristotle established the real state
of affairs
and determined the means of transforming clarity into
                                                    obscurity
and when laughter turned to rictus
and the word into a sword
pain already existed
Because the hand had long been modelled as a hand
and the word as a word
to expel evil from the world
But evil was within
even in the most exacting rules
and the most inevitable actions
And Dionysus drunk with wine and sun
had long been dancing round phallus and sword
forcing the plucked vermin to sing
And thus the song was born
While women veiled themselves in black
while towers burned and ships were sunk
and horses crushed the fruits of the earth
and the heart transformed itself into a dry crane
and blood left the body
That had no special links with heroism
nor the grief of loneliness nor the tears of deserted
                                                    hearths

Yet the old philosopher would even now invest
those butcheries with pretty rules
of the play
while the audience continues
to applaud death

Seeking the shore

I.

After the moonlit play of wind and night
all that remains is the green of olives
on the hillside
and the sonorous silence of scorpions

The sea has withdrawn into its mind
the wind is bored
the morning eager

The sun illumines
but a phantom landscape
the salty idyll of water and stone

Whiter now, lonely figure on the shore
with a barque's splinter in your eye
with a rock in your chest
with sterile ringing slivers of hoar-frost
all round you

II.

Be off be off now Ulysses
poor starry itinerant wage-slave
on the sea's waste-land

The sun's spider is trapping
the cricket's noisy panic
from the twisted trunks of the olive trees

The shore: neither song nor promise
under the milky haze of the grass
empty are the saddlebags of your palms

No waving hand   No bird depicts
the fall of bread
into the water's bubbles

Be off be off now
on the wage-slave's inevitable adventure
of the alien beauty of the sea

III.

Neither tempted nor tempter
Sweating travelling labourer
on the amorphous sea

Neither return nor departure
Pierced by the zenith's lance
in time's swamp

The salty wind licks
the exalted glance
Heavy are summer's chains

Yet invisible shores rise up
under the blood's thunder
that lights up the face

The sky a cupped hand the sea a drop
in the burden of memories
poor itinerant labourer of the sun

IV.

Yet there's one distant shore where I shall go
and there's a hill where I'll return one day
with the vanquished summer under the zenith's bleating

It gently opens under the blood's waterfall
in the humble sublimity of the sea

One shore one distant shore
carried in the saddlebag of a glance
from shore to shore carried one distant shore
yonder shore

Set off for it now set off for it Ulysses
The sterile rock of hoar-frost is blossoming
under the ringing shoots of your hands

Other Titles from
FOREST BOOKS

Special Collection

THE NAKED MACHINE Selected poems of Matthías Johannessen. Translated from the *Icelandic* by Marshall Brement. (Forest/ Almenna bokáfélagid)
0 948259 44 2 cloth £7.95   0 948259 43 4 paper £5.95   96 pages

ON THE CUTTING EDGE Selected poems of Justo Jorge Padrón. Translated from the *Spanish* by Louis Bourne.
0 948259 42 6 paper £7.95   176 pages

ROOM WITHOUT WALLS Selected poems of Bo Carpelan. Translated from the *Swedish* by Anne Born.
0 948259 08 6 paper £6.95   144 pages. Illustrated

CALL YOURSELF ALIVE? The love poems of Nina Cassian. Translated from the *Romanian* by Andrea Deletant and Brenda Walker. Introduction by Fleur Adcock.
0 948259 38 8 paper £5.95.   96 pages. Illustrated

RUNNING TO THE SHROUDS Six sea stories of Konstantin Stanyukovich.
Translated from the *Russian* by Neil Parsons.
0 948259 04 3 paper £5.95   112 pages. Illustrated

East European Series

FIRES OF THE SUNFLOWER Selected poems by Ivan Davidkov. Translated from the *Bulgarian* by Ewald Osers.
0 948 259 48 5 paper £6.95   96 pages. Illustrated

ARIADNE'S THREAD An anthology of contemporary Polish women poets. Translated from the *Polish* by Susan Bassnett and Piotr Kuhiwczak.
UNESCO collection of representative works.
0 948259 45 0 paper £6.95   96 pages.

POETS OF BULGARIA An anthology of contemporary Bulgarian poets.
Edited by William Meredith. Introduction by Alan Brownjohn.
0 948259 39 6 paper £6.95   112 pages.

THE ROAD TO FREEDOM Poems by Geo Milev. Translated from the *Bulgarian* by Ewald Osers.
UNESCO collection of representative works.
0 948259 40 X paper £6.95   96 pages. Illustrated

STOLEN FIRE Selected poems by Lyubomir Levchev.
Translated from the *Bulgarian* by Ewald Osers.
Introduction by John Balaban.
UNESCO collection of representative works.
0 948259 04 3 paper £5.95   112 pages. Illustrated

AN ANTHOLOGY OF CONTEMPORARY ROMANIAN POETRY
Translated by Andrea Deletant and Brenda Walker.
0 9509487 4 8 paper £5.00   112 pages.

GATES OF THE MOMENT Selected poems of Ion Stoica.
Translated from the *Romanian* by Brenda Walker and
Andrea Deletant. Dual text with cassette.
0 9509487 0 5 paper £5.00   126 pages   Cassette £3.50 plus VAT

SILENT VOICES An anthology of contemporary Romanian women
poets. Translated by Andrea Deletant and Brenda Walker.
0 948259 03 5 paper £6.95   172 pages.

EXILE ON A PEPPERCORN Selected poems of Mircea Dinescu.
Translated from the *Romanian* by Andrea Deletant and
Brenda Walker.
0 948259 00 0 paper £5.95.   96 pages. Illustrated.

LET'S TALK ABOUT THE WEATHER Selected poems of Marin Sorescu.
Translated from the *Romanian* by Andrea Deletant and
Brenda Walker.
0 9509487 8 0 paper £5.95   96 pages.

THE THIRST OF THE SALT MOUNTAIN Three plays by Marin Sorescu
(Jonah, The Verger, and the Matrix).
Translated from the *Romanian* by Andrea Deletant and
Brenda Walker.
0 9509487 5 6 paper £6.95   124 pages. Illustrated

VLAD DRACULA THE IMPALER A play by Marin Sorescu.
Translated from the *Romanian* by Dennis Deletant.
0 948259 07 8 paper £6.95   112 pages. Illustrated

Fun Series

JOUSTS OF APHRODITE Erotic poems collected from the Greek
Anthology Book V.
Translated from the *Greek* into modern English by Michael Kelly.
0 948259 05 1 cloth £6.95   0 94825 34 5 paper £4.95   96 pages